The Cross

The Cross

By
Barton Aaron Porter

E-BookTime, LLC
Montgomery, Alabama

The Cross

Library of Congress Control Number: 2007929225

ISBN: 978-1-59824-521-9

First Edition
Published June 2007
E-BookTime, LLC
6598 Pumpkin Road
Montgomery, AL 36108
www.e-booktime.com

Contents

Contents

Contents

Acknowledgments

I'd like to thank God the Father, the Almighty for forming man from the dust of the ground and breathing into his nostrils the breath of life.

I'd like to thank my Lord and Savior Jesus Christ for dying for my sins making it possible for me to have eternal life.

I'd like to thank the only three saints I've ever known: my mother Rosalie Porter, my mother-in-law Burdia Davis, and my mother-in-Christ Rosemary Cox for setting the example of holiness for me to try to follow.

I'd like to thank my dear friends The Hoovers: Stan, Almeter, Nigel, and Chelsea for opening up their home and giving me a place to perform my very first recital. Thank you all for making me *Famous For A Night.*

I'd like to thank all the people who came to that recital: Joe, Gene, Ally, Deborah, Janett, Naomi, Keren, Lamar, Robert, and all the other wonderful people who were there. You truly helped make that night a very special event and I will forever be grateful for your love and support.

I'd like to thank Kimberly Robb and Eleanor Cypress for two of the most beautiful smiles this world has ever seen. Ladies, thank you so much and please keep on smiling.

I'd like to thank Rachel and Ron for being my number one and two fans. I love you both may God Almighty look down and always smile on you and your children?

I want to thank all who have allowed me to share my art with them. There is truly nothing I love better than reciting my poems for people for what's an artist without a fan? I thank you all for purchasing my book and any future books I will have published. I hope you enjoy The Cross for it is my sole purpose to fill this world with my words.

Introduction

The title of this book comes from the single most important subject in this dying world. The cross is the only hope for mankind, not the cross in its self, but what took place upon it. You see Jesus shed his precious blood to open the floodgates of heaven that we might receive the blessing of eternal life. As of now, you and I are in a dying state. Every day here is just another step towards the grave. Only by receiving God's love gift can we escape the grip of death's cold hand. The cross of Jesus Christ is what inspired me to write this book and I hope it ministers to your soul as it does to mine. I love the Lord. He is the most important person there is. He is the creator of all things and the savior of the entire world.

I was a young man when I discovered that God had given me the gift to write and recite poetry. I had fallen madly in love with a lady who belonged to the Seventh-day Adventist Church. I don't think I ever had such feelings for anyone. There were so many wonderful words that needed to come out, so therefore, I decided to express what I was feeling in a poem. She was very impressed, but unfortunately she was moving away. I was crushed when she left town, but all wasn't lost. You see that was when I discovered the skill of my pen. I was curious, could I write with the same passion for Christ? I thought surely I could. I mean, after all, he is the true love of my life, that is, the one who literally died so I could live. Therefore, I quickly settled it in my heart that I would do a book of poems dedicated to the cross.

You see Jesus is the most important person in the Trinity as far as man is concerned. It was he who came forth leaving the glory of heaven behind, becoming what he himself had a part in creating for the purpose of saving us from the anxiously waiting hands of hell. We were drowning in a sea of suffering, sickness, and shame until Christ came. There was no hope for man but then God threw us a life preserver. You see Jesus Christ is our lifesaver and it's up us to reach out and take hold of his cross.

What Jesus accomplished on the cross no one else could. It was the single greatest act of love God has ever shown to man.

About the Author

Barton Aaron Porter was born October 14, 1967 in Chicago, Illinois. He is the sixth son of the eight boys of Thomas and Rosalie Porter. He was raised on the Southside not far from a poverty-stricken slum. However, having very generous Aunts he had the things that every child should have. Barton has always been involved in some kind of writing ever since he was a child. As a youth he would draw his own comic books and write the storyline for them just like Marvel Comics. As a teen he was a songwriter and lyricist to the extent that he even once recorded a song. It wasn't until much later, that he would find his true calling.

Barton wasn't like most urban African American children. You see what appeared outwardly to be a normal child was just a smoke screen hiding the truth. Barton always knew there was more to what we see through our human eyes, and he started searching for the answers to certain questions at a very young age. Those questions being: Why are we here? Why do we die? How can we avoid death? Why is there so much suffering in this world? The answers would come years later at the tender age of 19. A car crash in which he was involved would be the turning point in his life.

Understanding had he died he would've been lost for all eternity Barton started searching for Jesus Christ. He looked in many cathedrals and other religious institutions, but Christ wasn't there. It wasn't until he opened the Bible that he would find what he was looking for. You see God is not far from any of us and through his written word he has provided us with the answers to many questions.

I, Barton Aaron Porter, now know the answers to those questions and this book of Christian poetry is a gift from God through me to you. May the good Lord bless you and keep you all the years of your life.

Love, Minister Barton Aaron Porter

A Conversation With God

I was having a conversation with God
The man sitting next to me didn't understand.
He really thought that this was odd
Because he didn't know the creator of man.

I was thanking God for all the things he'd done
Like my home, food, clothes, and health.
But most of all for sending His Son,
So I could avoid "The Second Death!"

I said, "Thank you Lord for watching over me
When I wasn't even serving you.
And thank you Lord for my family
The old members and the new."

I said, "Thank you Lord Jesus for the victory.
You brought at the cross of Christ!
And thank you for allowing me
To picture me living eternal life."

And when I finished our conversation
I didn't care if he found it odd.
And now I say to all creation,
"When was the last time you had a talk with God?"

A Little Place We Call Earth

It was prophesied in the scriptures
That a virgin would have a child.
When the angel named Gabriel confirmed this picture
The Virgin Mary wore a smile.

It was said her son would be a prophet,
Our high priest, savior, and king.
When the shepherds heard this topic
The heavens opened where angels sing.

It was foretold he'd do many miracles
And still be rejected by most all men.
You see they couldn't discern what was spiritual
When Jesus died to take away their sin.

It was spoken by Isaiah the prophet
That he would suffer in humiliation.
And there was nothing that could stop it.
It was necessary to save all nations.

It was written he would die for the human race
Before his mother gave birth.
And all to save a little place
That we call the earth.

A Message To The Devil

While I was sitting silently inside the walls of a chapel;
It didn't matter they thought the fruit she ate was an apple.
As I read of how you tried to ruin mankind's future
I thought no wonder The Father had to boot you.

How dare you slap The Creator's hand
And beguile the mother of truth.
How dare you! You must be an insane man
Or some kind of maniac on the loose.

But what I don't understand is why with you so many ran.
You must be quite a charlatan, my man.
I mean to be able to talk a third
Of God's angels into fighting a war they couldn't win.
I must say, that's pretty good,
To get all those angels to volunteer to be firewood.

But your very own light blinded your sight and sealed your fate.
And that's not too bright. Now is it, Sate?
Think about it! How could one fly above the Most High?
Even you had to know that was a lie.

He made you the most coveted Cherub when you were nothing!
Think about it! You were nothing and He made you something.
So where's the appreciation coming from the creation?
I mean come on! You were there when He made the dawn.

You saw God make the stars,
So how did you ever figure that they were yours?
Now the door has been shut to you up in Heaven,
Yet you still continue to make the dough rise like leaven.

When will you learn?
Will it be on the day when you start to burn?
You're just a mental patient in a straight jacket
Locked in a padded cell and after one thousand years.
You're going to spend eternity in Hell!

A Second Chance

I stayed in a coma for seven years as stiff as a board
As still as a chair with little to no sign of life whatsoever.
Even doctors when asked, "Will he recover?"
Answered, "Probably never."

People use to look at me and wonder;
What had he done to anger the God of thunder?

"What crime had he committed?" they'd say,
"That was deserving of this kind of punishment?"
"It must've been some great crime," they'd say,
"Something like overthrowing the government."

Then my doctor came rushing to my room
As the light shined in my window from a full moon.

Then an amazing thing happened to me that night;
My eyes were opened and I could see this shiny light.
Then these little strange gray images
Started to appear before my sight.

My hearing wasn't as clear as it could be,
But I could hear these funny sounding little voices,
Asking me, "Can you hear me? Can you hear me?"

Then suddenly the picture became clear
And I could see the doctor and the nurses standing near.
That's when I heard them cheer
As from my eyes came the most grateful tears.

You see God had given me a second chance;
I saw His angel when he appeared.

A Woman Called Wisdom

You could see the signs of age and time
In the wrinkles in her skin.
But her expression said everything was fine
As she sang of how Christ wins.

She rocked back and forth in her rocking chair
Without a single care in this world.
Every time Church opened she was there
Ever since she was a girl.

She took heed to her Pastor's sermons,
And in her heart, she hid God's words.
She ignored the silly antics of her brother Sherman
Who didn't pay attention to a word he heard.

Then later, in life, those lessons he missed
On Sherman would take their toll.
It was then he would come to his big Sis'
And by her, he would find his true role.

But his smile wasn't the only one she would tighten;
You see she was a well that would never run dry.
A woman called wisdom will always enlighten
Because she is the Word of God from up high.

Adam's Sin

She couldn't resist when she saw the fruit
Hanging from the knowledge tree.
The enemy was at the root
Saying, "God doesn't want you to see."

So she took the fruit then took a bite
To remove from her mind all doubt.
But the devil knew they'd still be alright
Until the fruit was found in Adam's mouth.

So Satan sent the fruit to Adam through Eve
So he couldn't see through this paradox.
But the fruit wasn't all that he received;
He now held the keys to Pandora's Box.

You see what she did didn't really matter
Cause he was the one God held accountable.
But both of their dreams were quickly shattered;
When they were told from the garden they had to go.

Then war, poverty, and corruption
Entered into the world of men.
You see the whole system malfunctioned
All because of Adam's sin.

All We Need To Win Is The Lord

As he stood towering over the others on the battlefield
The spirit of fear appeared
And contaminated all who stood near.

Then along came this little ruddy colored shepherd boy
Who spoke of how this giant
The Lord by him would soon destroy.

The giant made his challenge
And all but the shepherd boy did flee.
He said, "Who sent this great elephant
This annoying little flea?"

The shepherd said, "You come to me wearing armor
With a huge shield and sword.
But I come to you in the name of the Almighty Lord."

Goliath rushed upon him as little David ran his way.
He whirled his sling beside him and its stone went not astray.

The stone flew nice and high
And it struck him right between his eyes.
He fell down to his knees then in the earth his face did fly.

Then the shepherd ran upon him
And quickly grabbed his sword.
Then he chopped off his head
And from his neck the red blood poured.

You see all we need to win is the Lord.

Another Day

Unseen events befall us all;
Regardless, if we're great or small.

A rich man died and left his fifty "mil" to no one;
He had no idea that at thirty-one he'd be done.

A poor man died and nobody even cared
That fifty million with this poor man the rich should've shared.

Because the angel of death wears a long black robe
That has a big black hood.
And he roams the streets of the slums.
And the private neighborhoods in Hollywood.

He carries a razor sharp sickle
As he roams throughout the land
And he takes away the life of a man
With a single touch of his hand.

So we must go on living
Never being quite sure
Of that day when death will come
And knock upon our door.

So every time you open your eyes
This is what you should say,
"I thank you Lord
For letting me live to see another day;"

Another Night

The clouds of depression
Are hovering over my head above.
The thick arms of aggression
Are smothering the emotion love.

The white teeth of demons are glistening
As they whisper things in my ears.
I'm hearing but not listening
As my eyes fight back the tears.

The whirlwind of confusion
Is spinning round full of dread.
They're sending in delusion
Trying to get inside my head.

The pressure and pain
Is pumping like blood through my veins.
As I fight to remain
Right here among the sane.

I'm handcuffed to the pier
As on my neck stands up the hair.
The stress and the fear
Is just too much for me to bear.

So I grab my pen tight
Sit in my den and I start to write.
If it wasn't for Christ
I couldn't make it through another night.

Arise

When Jesus came near the city gate.
He saw a dead man being carried out.
He was the only child of his mother.
There was not another soul in her house.

When Jesus saw her, he had compassion on her,
And told her not to weep.
Then he reached out and touched the stretcher
Being carried by the men in the street.

Then the young man who lay dead
Opened up his eyes.
When he heard the voice of Jesus say,
"Arise!"

Beast And Man

The long white beard of Jehovah
Hung from His chin as He slowly leaned over.
His fiery eyes were opened as the nations He starts to seek.
He's like a silent giant that lives in the skies and never sleeps.

He just watches as He sits there in the air,
So quiet that some doubt He's even there.

But there will come a day
When this great king will make His way
Back here to earth and this time to stay.

He will descend upon Jerusalem to join the Son of Man,
And then the Jews once again will have their land
Because God will dwell forever with beast and man.

Then men will come from many nations
To learn the ways of peace from this great king;
After all, He is their Savior, and as God He knows all things.

A river of crystal clear water will flow from Jehovah's Throne
To give drink to all the nations and to keep green the things
He has grown.

And the sound of peace will echo across the land
Because He will be everything to beast and man.

Demons

It's easier to see what's on the surface
Than it is to see what's on the bottom.
Yeah, he pulled the trigger but it was demons
That motivated the man who shot him.

You see they have been pulling the strings
From behind the scenes for years.
They're like Gremlins
Who whisper wicked things in our ears.

The murders, the rapes, the wars, and the debates
Is all the devil's angels' handiwork.
You see every time they get us to do their will.
They snicker and wear a smirk.

They work 24 hours a day, 7 days a week
Because they have already been condemned.
You see they can't be forgiven for their sins
So they want us to go to hell just like them.

And they will be doing these things
Until the end of this age.
If you want to take a look at them,
Pick up your Bible, and turn a page.

Earth's King

I have the ability to be invisible;
Although, I have no wings I can fly.
I can walk right through walls
And I will never die.

I'm the world's fastest splinter;
I can travel at the speed of light.
I'm the world's greatest athlete
So I will never lose a fight.

I will and can go the distance;
I refuse to fail the test.
I won't allow anything to stop me
Because I am the best.

What I am is man!
I am earth's king
And with God on my side
I can do anything!

Fornication

She came riding in a chariot
Being pulled by six naked men.
Those idiots were willing to carry it
Cause she had gotten control of them.

She wore a see-through nightgown
And had a red rose in her hair.
When she entered the town every faithful clown
Went out and had an affair.

She opened her gates as wide as a lake
And the whole crowd rushed right in.
She's the addiction we couldn't shake
Cause she's the queen of all sexual sins.

She's a thick dark cloud
Overshadowing every nation.
She's the talk of the crowd
And her name is Fornication.

Get Up

There once was a Christian who walked with God.
The devil came tripped him up and he fell.

But he didn't get up and continue his walk
So he died and he went straight to hell.

So if you fall down to the ground.
Get up!

Glory

As I struggle to escape from the cocoon of society.
The pressures, pains, and heartaches come in a variety.
I was born in the womb of darkness
Wrapped with the finest threads of bondage
I cried for help to no avail.
You see I was trapped inside the mouth of hell.

So I started forcing my elbows and arms against the wall
To make room for me to crawl down hell's hall.
And as I did I experienced a change.
A strange metamorphosis had begun.
The earth above me cracked and I saw the sun.

So I scratched a bigger hole in the earth that covered me.
I was a drop of light, which to me was a new discovery.
Then I exploded from the ground like a mine
That had been stepped on.
I looked beneath my feet at the brown bag I crept upon.
I noticed I was no longer light-green, ugly, and fat.
I was now very lean, lovely, and black.

And on my back there were two leaf-like wings.
Two of the most beautiful works of art this world had ever seen.
One was like the many colors of a rainbow.
The other looked like the painted face of a Navajo.
At that moment I realized the moral of the story.
After the struggle comes the glory!

God Can Slay A Thousand Men

He was confronted by a host of a thousand Philistine men.
This military might that came to fight just knew they'd win,
So with anger in their eyes.
They came in on every side.
He had to think fast.
He saw the jawbone of an ass.

They all tried to rush him
As he stooped down to the ground.
They thought surely we will crush him,
But he turned that all around.

They attacked him from the left side
And they attacked him from the right.
None of them was frightened;
They were all brave men of fight.

But one by one
The thousand fell dead without a sound.
Then Samson stood upon the men
He had piled up in a mound.

He held up that blood soaked bone,
Which he held tightly in his grasp,
And yelled, "God can slay a thousand men
With the jawbone of an ass!"

God Is

God is the water in your glass
And the food upon your plate.
God is the one we should ask
Before it's just too late.

God is the health you have
Enjoyed for all of these years.
Because God is your true dad
He'll take away your fears.

God is the house you live in.
He's the shelter you enjoy.
God is the one who died for your sin.
The restorer of peace and joy.

God is that miracle
That took your cancer away.
You see God is more than spiritual
He's the one and only way.

God is the water in your glass
And the food upon your plate.
God is the one we should ask
Before it's just too late.

God Is Good

Father if I had a thousand tongues
I still couldn't praise you enough.
You've walked with me when old and young
Whenever things got tough.

You helped me when I couldn't.
You made me believe I could
And that is why I have to say,
"God is good!"

Father if I sang you a thousand hymns
That still wouldn't be enough.
You've always helped The Tiny Tim's
And made sure they had their stuff.

You helped me when I wouldn't.
If I could you knew I would
And that is why I have to say,
"God is good!"

Father if I danced for you a thousand times
That still wouldn't be enough.
You've forgiven me crime after crime.
You've always cleaned me up.

You helped me when I was bad.
You forgave my being a hood
And that is why I have to say,
"God is good!"

God's Superman

He wrestled with the wild beasts at Ephesus
And with God's help he would prevail.
He sang praises to that very God
As he sat in the darkness of his cell.

He had the zeal of the raging fire
And the will of solid steel.
He found favor in the eyes of Messiah
On his way to Christian kill.

A whole day and a night
He spent out in the deep.
His body was freezing cold
But in his soul was warmth and peace.

He was stoned on one occasion
And left in the streets to die.
It was there he was caught up to the third heaven
To meet God in the sky.

He was beaten with whips.
He was beaten with rods.
And all this he suffered
For his love of the Lamb of God.

But he was no ordinary man.
He was a Hebrew scholar of law.
I'm talking about the greatest Christian soldier of them all.
God's superman the apostle He called Paul.

Goodtime Charlie

He just couldn't wait to get his hands on her.
She was the goodtime Charlie had to have,
But what he didn't know was that this pro would be his last.

So he grabbed her and held her with all of his might.
He rocked her and rolled her all through the night.
He said, it was good, and this he said, twice.
He growled at her thrice and he gave her a bite.

He screamed, "More, more, more, sin is so nice!"
He forgot all he heard about the Lord Jesus Christ.
He jerked to the left.
He jerked to the right,

Something popped,
His heart stopped,
Then out went his lights.
And now down in hell he regrets the whole night.

But he just couldn't wait to get his hands on her.
She was the goodtime Charlie had to have,
But what he didn't know was that this pro would be his last.

Heaven

As I sit here seeking inspiration for another poem.
I can wish all I want, but still my friends are gone.
It's dawn now but soon the night will fall.
As I call not one of you can hear me at all.

So why am I in misery?
It was God who promised eternity.
And deep in my soul
I know it shall be.

Besides, what other choices do I really have?
I mean, what else is there for me to grab?
Heaven must be true!
Up there is a world beyond the tent of blue.

And we came here from there.
Sometimes things are so obvious and yet we're still unaware.
Have you ever stared at the sun's glare on the water of the lake?
You see two worlds at once and neither one of them are fake.

Because if you jumped into the water
You would enter without a swirl.
Heaven is on the outside of this world.

He Who Sat In Darkness

He who sat in darkness
Heard the noise of a great crowd.
It was like the rumbling of thunder
Behind the thunderclouds.

So he asked, "What did this mean?"
They said, "The prophet was passing by."
"Son of David! Have mercy on me!"
The blind man started to cry.

The blind man kept calling him
Till Jesus said, "Bring him here."
He felt the excitement of anticipation
As his disciples brought him near.

Jesus asked, "What do you want me to do?"
He answered, "Lord, let me receive my sight!"
Then he who sat in darkness saw a great light
Because the first face he saw was Jesus Christ's.

His Love For Us Was Real

He saw their smiling faces
As they led him to his doom.
He showed us what true grace is
As he traveled to the tomb.

Those Roman soldiers mocked him
And his people did the same.
But none of these things shocked him.
You see to die was why he came.

His back bled red with blood.
His body dripped wet with sweat.
His feet trudged through the mud
But in his heart was no regret.

He would often fall to the ground
Underneath the weight of the cross.
But he refused to stay down
Cause he had come to save the lost.

Then he died for the human race
Upon that lonely hill.
You see Jesus took our place
Because his love for us was real.

His Name Is Jesus Christ

He is the Fountain of Living Water.
The Rose of Sharon and the Lily of the Valley.
He is the One who rose
From the grave after Calvary.

He is the Bright and Morning Star
And the Prince of the kings of earth.
He is Alpha and Omega.
The Last and First.

He is the Shepherd of the sheep.
The Resurrection and the Ransom Price.
He is the Door
That opens to the road to Paradise.

He is the Savior of the world.
The Way.
The Truth.
The Life.

And if you know not of whom I speak
His name is Jesus Christ.

H.I.V.

I am the enforcer of God's law.
I'll get the attention of them all.
They won't forever ignore me.

I am the Cancer that can't be cured.
I am the answer. Yes, I'm sure.
I am the end of infidelity.

I am the meat grinder of gay boys and girls.
I am the ruin of the promiscuous world.
God said, "Marry or let it be."

I am the destroyer of free sex.
I am the bonfire that burns that text.
Don't stand there, asking, who is he?

I am the wrath of Almighty God.
I am the thunder, lightening, and clouds.
No one on earth will escape from me.

Across the country I bring the plague.
I am the anger of God, His rage.
By the way, my name is H.I.V.

Hold On

When the voices of devils call
We mustn't ever answer.
Because sin dwells within our skin
Just like Cancer.

When dark angels stand at your side
Egging you on to be evil's pawn.
You must hold onto what's right
Until they've gone.

Because hell has enlarged herself
To accommodate her new inmates.
You see the wrong road is being chosen
At an alarming rate.

There will be very few
Who will be allowed to stroll through Heaven's gate.
Because it's what you do
That shows if you truly have faith.

So when the hour of temptation comes
With all your might you must hold on.
Because the battle isn't over till it's won.
So what I say to you, I say to all, "Hold on!"

How I Became The Lord's Poet

The Lord said I could be His poet
If I gave Him all the praise.
So I bowed to my Lord Jehovah
And both hands to Him I raised.

He said, "A poet is not an entertainer
But a poet is like a preacher.
A poet is an idea changer
Because a poet is a teacher."

He said, "A poet can take the world on a ride
And cause them to see it through his eyes.
A poet can see through Satan's disguise.
Therefore, a poet exposes all lies."

He said, "A poet can write his heart down
Upon a piece of paper.
Then make it come alive
Like the sun makes water vapor.

Because a poet is an artist
Whom God has given a gift."
God said, "Always use your gift
To encourage and uplift."

He said, "If you do I will walk with you
And I will make your name great.
And I will use your mouth to bear witness
In every place."

So I said, "I will!" and then stood still.
And the most high God bestowed my skill.

I Am You

I use to stand in the presence of the great white throne.
I use to dwell in the glow of the eternal home.
Then war broke out among the citizens of heaven.
The angels fought with all kinds of ancient weapons.

I chose the wrong side which angered the most high
And to that world I had to say, goodbye.
Now here I am among the children of a lesser world
Just another mortal like every boy and girl.

I now know what it is to feel pain.
I now know what it is to cry.
And one day I will no longer remain.
Because soon I will know what it is to die.

You see I didn't appreciate the world from which I fell.
Now I've been imprisoned in this fleshly prison cell.
I now walk in a state of blue.
Although, you don't believe me this story is true.

So who am I?
I am you!

I Can Do All Things

The odds are against me. This is true.
It's been this way for years. This is nothing new,
So I can't allow myself to be intimidated by what I hear and see.
I can do all things through Christ who strengthens me.

They are united and they have many.
We have very little and they have plenty,
But I can't allow myself to be intimidated by what I hear and see.
I can do all things through Christ who strengthens me.

The world was against me before I was even born.
I've seen the lives that this wicked world has torn,
But I can't allow myself to be intimidated by what I hear and see.
I can do all things through Christ who strengthens me.

The master led the way when He went to Calvary,
And after day three the whole world He made free.
So I can't allow myself to be intimidated by what I hear and see.
I can do all things through Christ who strengthens me.

44

I Know A Better Way

I watch them as they walk right by me everyday.
They can't hear me when I say, I know a better way.
I watch them suffer needlessly. I want to help them be okay,
But they won't come my way.
When I say, I know a better way.

The false prophets have deceived them
And turned them all away.
Some are chasing fame,
Some seeking lust, and some big pay.

I saw a woman who was addicted to sex.
It's been fifty years this day
But the cars no longer stop to pick her up.
Because now she's old and gray.

One day she just dropped right on the block
Down to her knees to pray.
I stepped forward when she saw me,
I said, "Don't be afraid. Just stay."

She looked at me and said, "Who are you?"
I said, "My name is Jesus and I am the Way."

She said, "Lord, I'm not worthy, please just go away."
I said, "Your sins I have forgiven. Your sins I've washed away.
Come with me my daughter. Come with me today.

Just trust me!
Believe in me!
I know a better way!"

I Should've Been Talking To God

Man, I've been wearing out my peer's ears for years
With the problems I have had.
Telling them about my fears and doubts
And the things that make me sad.

I thought that this would help me
But it didn't do the job.
Right then and there it dawned on me
I should've been talking to God.

Man, I've been using my ink to record what I think
Every night inside my bedroom lab.
Just filled with rage filling up each page
Then tearing them from the tab.

I thought that this would help me
But this too soon seemed to be odd.
I mean why was I just sitting there?
When I should've been talking to God.

I Will

Jesus told him to tell no one what he had done,
Saying, "Only go offer what's required by law."
But to the joy this leper felt he would soon succumb
And the good news he would spread to all.

He didn't mean to disobey the words of his Lord.
If he could have he would have kept it to himself.
But when he saw his skin had been fully restored
To celebrate was all he had left.

You see he would never forget this deed done by the Son;
How after he made his request he stood there to be healed.
Then Jesus touched him with four fingers and his thumb
But only after, he said to him, "I will."

If We Would Only Listen

If we would only listen
We'd avoid a lot of pain.
If we would only listen
We would drive Satan insane.

If we would only listen
We would never fail a test.
If we would only listen
All our lives we would be blessed.

If we would only listen
We would never take a lost.
If we would only listen
We would benefit from the cross.

If we would only listen
There'd be peace throughout the land.
If we would only listen
To God instead of man.

I'm Not Like You

You assume we're all the same
But please don't say my name.
I'm not like you. I'm unique.

You say all people are the same
As though this were some kind of game,
But I'm a Christian. I'm not a freak.

You say everybody does it
But let me tell you something cousin.
I don't smoke, use drugs, or drink.

You say we're all going to burn in hell.
Then I say, please don't tell that tale
Because I know I'm going up in a blink.

You say nobody can really live
The way God said to live.
Well, I say, you better take a close look at me.

You say heaven isn't real.
You only go around once so get your thrills
But there's more to life than the eye can see.

You assume we're all the same
But please don't say my name.
I'm not like you. I'm unique.

You see I believe in his holy name
And the gift of life I have claimed.
I don't know about you,
But I'm going to meet the Prince of peace.

It Is Done

At the foot of the cross stood Mary
And among Jesus' disciples was his favorite one.
Jesus looking at John said, "Behold your mother."
Then looking at her, he said, "Woman, behold your son."

The sin debt of the world he had just paid off.
You see before the battle had begun Jesus won.
That's why the last words he would speak from the cross
Would simply be the words, it is done.

It's A Good Thing I'm Not God

They break the rules
They expect others to live by.
They head for their private pools
As they drive by the homeless guy.

They swear on the Bible
Then lie like there is no God.
They focus on their courtroom rivals.
Then at night, they say, "It's just my job."

They go to see their mistress
At least once or twice a week.
They come home and kiss their missus
And then say, "Boy, am I beat!"

They steal taxpayers' money
To buy their mistress a shiny ring.
They think it's really funny
But in the fires of hell they'll all soon sing.

They lay down every night
Without ever kneeling down to pray.
They could care less about Jesus Christ
And the price he had to pay.

Then they have to nerve to say that this life is hard.
Well, it's a good thing for them I'm not God.

Jealousy

He just stood there watching
As the fires of acceptance consumed his brother's sacrifice.
He was told that he too, would be accepted, if he did better,
But he wouldn't take the Father's advice.

So he said to his brother,
"Let us go out into the field."
When Abel walked two steps ahead of him
A voice said to Cain, "Kill!"

And that was the first time
A man's blood had been spilled.
Jealousy is a disease
That makes the mind ill.

Kindness To A Stranger

He lay there in the road as a victim of an attack.
His body was cold as his head bled red in back.
His wallet was gone and he was far from his home.
He was alone. It was as though he was on his own.

Then a priest came by and saw him lying as he died
But he didn't help the guy he just walked to the other side.
Then a Levite came nigh and saw the same dying guy
But he like the priest just left him there to die.

Then a Samaritan saw the man
And quickly to the man he ran.
He tended to his wounds
Then he took him to a nice warm room.

The man who owned the Inn
Asked him, if he was his friend.
He said he didn't know the man.
He was just lending him a helping hand.

That's when the Innkeeper blew,
"Why do you do these things you do?"
He said, "Because Jesus said, 'Do
Unto others as you'd have them do for you!'"

Knowing Christ

They sang and shouted
But they didn't really know anything about it.
They danced and clapped
Without knowing the facts.

They said, "Amen!"
But they didn't really understand.
They said, "This was nice!"
Without knowing Christ.

Lies

The devil said, "You won't surely die
God is holding back something from you, my girl."
You see all it took was just one lie
To ruin the entire world.

God had warned them not to eat
Said this fruit would cause them to die.
But the serpent convinced her with his speech
Introduced the world to its very first lie.

Today tall tales come in a variety
Some in the form of exaggerations and alibi's.
And within certain circles of our society.
They're even getting paid to tell lies.

But the Bible says, every idle word you speak
Comes to God's ears like you're wearing a wire.
And that the flames of hell will make a breach
To consume every single liar.

Yet everyday we lie under God's roof
Knowing it was a lie that caused the fall.
My point is if you can't tell the truth
You shouldn't say anything at all.

Life Without Christ

He forced his way pass me.
He took a chance on losing his life.

He blew his horn as he drove pass.
He really thought that he was right.

Some people would call him crazy.
Some would argue he wasn't too bright

But what he did didn't faze me
Because he hadn't seen the light.

You see he was just another example of what I call
Life without Christ.

Love {The World's Strongest Emotion}

Kindness had him open his door to the poor
But lust had him out seeking another score.
Anger had him hit a guy in the eye.
Sarcasm had him make his wise guy reply.

Fear had him worried about the coming revenge
And guilt made him tilt. It almost did him in.
Greed helped him succeed and still want more and more.
Gluttony made him eat meat till the pants he wore tore.

Rage turned the page
And handed him the twelve gauge.
Then fame claimed his name
And put him on the front stage.

Regret caused him to sweat
And toss and turn in his bed.
Then perversion filled his mind
With big bust and long legs.

Then love came from up above
And cried out to all the lost.
You see it was love that paid the cost
When Jesus died on the cross.

And that's when from my mind
Was removed any notion
That "Love" is the world's strongest emotion.

Man I'm Really Glad Jesus Came

When God sent the Savior into the World
That's when Heaven gave Earth
Its most precious Pearl.

When the Lamb came
And Died for Us on the Cross.
That's when Salvation came to the Lost.

When Messiah rose three days later from the Grave
That's when Death and Hell
Had to free its Slaves.

And now as Kings and Priests
With the Christ we'll Reign.
Man, I'm really glad Jesus came.

Messiah

They lied when they brought him before
Some sort of kangaroo night court.
They said there was no need to hear anymore
So they brought him before the governor's porch.

Where they falsely accused him
Until he was sentenced to be put to death.
Then they mocked him and abused him
But he wasn't concerned for himself.

The soldiers made a crown with thorns as sharp as nails
Which pierced into his head.
Then they beat him with a cat of nine tails
Until his back was cut to shreds.

They then laid him on a torturing stake before both old and young
As they drove those rusty strikes through his wrists and feet.
Then facing the sun is how he was hung
Right there in the burning desert heat.

Where he died for us fornicators, us thieves, murderers, and liars
So the kingdom of heaven we could all acquire.
He saved us from that burning lake of fire
Because Jesus of Nazareth was the Messiah!

No Neutral Ground

I could see them staring out
Through the eyes of the people they possessed.
I didn't know what this was about
At that time I was a mess.

I would feeling this tingling sensation
Every time one would come near.
At home or at the station
I was in a constant state of fear.

This drove me into the Bible
I searched the scriptures for an answer.
Meanwhile the Lord's true rival
Had his way with me like Cancer.

Years later I would discover
God wasn't pleased with me.
That's why my heavenly brother
Let Satan cause me this misery.

You see I wasn't on that Christian level
Because from time to time I'd still let him down.
You see you're either with God or the devil
Because there is no neutral ground.

Oh Why Did He Tamper With The Creation?

The dark sky looked like a black rug
With shiny little diamonds scattered all over it.
The sun looked like it had been hand spun
With fire coming from inside of its orbit.

The shooting stars raced across the skies
Like fire flies fleeing from a surprise.
As the planet Saturn stood still in the midst of a ring of fire.
Yes it was the Messiah that created all that he did desire.

The angels sang like a nest of newborn baby birds
With their golden wings towering above.
The enemy stood ignoring the meaning of their words
As he plotted his evil scheme against the God of love.

He looked into his mirror and became his own hero.
He became the apple of his eye.
He continued to fan the flames of his insanity
Until he uttered the words, "I will be like the most high!"

And to unity, peace, and prosperity
The world had to say, "Goodbye!"
"Oh why did he have to tamper with the creation?
Why? Why? Why?"

Only Grace Can Win The Race

You can pray until you're old and gray
And you still won't be okay.

You can tithe for all twelve tribes
And you still might not survive.

You can attend Church and read every verse
But only Jesus can make the last be first.

You can do good in the whole neighborhood
And still find yourself lost in the woods.

You see you can talk until you're blue in the face
But only grace can win the race!

Only Jesus Can Make It Right

I remember a time when we stood on the steps
Of this nation's Capitol demanding our equal rights.
We gained but what we gained came with a price.
Over a million black lives had to be sacrificed
Just so we could have the same rights as these whites.
We gained one kind of freedom,
But we lost another during our fight.
You see all around town blacks are now looking down,
Saying, "Your skin is too dark and mines is just right."

As a sister struts her stuff switching her big butt from left to right.
A fool smoking a kool who dropped out of school
Is looking for a fight.
And not too far outside of a bar
A gang sign gets thrown up in his sight.
What in the world happened to the blacks' insight?
How did the people get filled with so much envy, hate, and spite?
I think it was the day they got away from Jesus Christ.

You see instead of Jesus Christ.
They started hanging out late at night.
Smoking weed, drinking wine and beer
Staying up until the morning light.
That's when the neighborhood lost its heroes.
There are no more upright knights.
This is what has happened to the black communities' might.
We need to get back to Christ
Cause only Jesus can make it right.

Our Friendship Will Never End

Here lays an example of what we all should be.
A wonderful woman full of loving kindness,
Compassion, and beauty.

A gentle soul full of warmth and love
Who shined like the purest gold.
A hand to hold, a friend of old who knew no cold.

A Christian who completed the mission we call "Faith!"
We love you and we will miss you dear sister saint.

Now sleep Burdia Davis until the last trumpet sounds
Until the dead rebounds at the trumpet's sound
To all head uptown.

And then we will be together again my friend.
But this time our friendship will never end.

I'm honored that I knew you Burdy.
Your courage taught me how to be sturdy.
Your strength inspired me not to yield.
Your peaceful way showed us how to live.

You were a soft caterpillar
Who was bound to change and fly.
So I won't cry for now
I'll just say, goodbye.

Because I know that I will see your face again.
And when I do our friendship will never end.

Our Mission

The most difficult and worthwhile thing
That any of us will ever do is become a Christian.
You see this and this alone is our mission.

Paradise

He hung next to our savior.
He changed his behavior.
He turned his head to him
Seeking his favor.

He rebuked the fool on the other side.
He dropped his pride
And gave it his last try.
He opened his mouth and then he cried,

"Lord, please remember me,
When you come into your kingdom."
He knew although, they were going to die
Back from the dead Jesus could bring them.

He confessed to Christ
All the sins of his life.
Then Jesus said,
"You will be with me in paradise."

People Who Live In Glass Houses

There before the judge stood
The madam of the "You know what house!"
And right beside the madam
Our former mayor and his spouse.

The judge looked at the mayor
And slowly shook his head.
"And to think you were our mayor!"
The judge sarcastically said.

Then the judge yelled, "Guilty!"
As he slammed his gavel down.
Then as he walked to his chambers
A little photo fell from his gown.

As the attorneys all looked at it
Their minds just drew a blank.
It was the picture of a prostitute
And the judge being spanked.

People who live in glass houses
Shouldn't throw stones
Until you correct what's wrong with your life.
Leave my life alone.

Pray

The demons are all around me
Applying pressure in every way.
One thing we can say about them
Is they really earn their pay.

They're whispering in my ears
All kinds of negative stuff.
They're strengthening my fears
Trying to make my life real tough.

But I'm holding onto God's hand.
Holding on with all I've got.
I'm trusting the Son of Man
Trying to ruin the devil's plot.

The angel of the Lord is with me
To keep me in the way.
You see God will not forget thee
If you'll just kneel down and pray.

So when things aren't going your way just kneel down and pray.
And when things are okay still kneel down and pray.
Because God and God alone is our hope and our stay.
You want Satan to go away then just kneel down and pray!

Pride

Sir Charles Winchester was a very proud man.
He wore a thirty thousand dollar diamond ring on his hand.
He flirted and flaunted with the upper echelon.
He got nominated for the Peace prize and just knew he won.

As Winchester awaited a certain telephone call.
He heard the phone ringing then stood proud and tall.
Then he turned to his butler to receive the good news
But at first to speak up the butler refused.

Winchester got frustrated as his butler procrastinated.
He inhaled then yelled, "Filbert? Tell me, if I made it!"
When Filbert dropped his head he was instantly hated.
Then finally, he opened his mouth and just said it.

"I'm sorry Winchester, but the man said who called.
It's my great displeasure to tell you. You weren't nominated at all."
As Winchester sank in his recliner feeling quite appalled.
He recalled the scriptures say, when pride comes then comes a fall.

Repent

Once I realized I had gotten off track.
I knew immediately that I had to get back.

So I rolled out of bed onto my knees.
Then said, "Father, please? Forgive me, please?"

Then suddenly, I felt the sweet peace of relief
Which came as a result of my sincere belief.

You see there's only one thing you can do when you sin.
And that's repent and then try not to do it again.

Restore

As he spoke in the ears of his audience
Mental pictures formed in their heads.
Then a fire started burning inside their hearts
And alive became the dead.

He was quite a sight to look at.
His garment was very rare.
You could tell he was a Nazarite
By the long locks of his hair.

He lived alone in the wilderness.
He caught locust for his food.
It was out there in the wilderness.
The prophet taught his school.

He was as bold as a lion
When he witnessed they all did hear.
He brought comfort to the people
And to the king he brought fear.

When the people asked him who he was
This was his reply.
"There comes one after me
Whose shoe latchet I can't untie!"

He looked at the people then said of the man upon the shore.
"Behold the lamb of God that takes away the sin of the world!"
Then John said, "I have come to call you
But He came to restore!"

Savior Lord And King

I heard a lady talking about
What her diamond ring was worth.
I started to turn and shout
It's just another rock that came from the earth.

Today, I heard a man say, "I earn my pay!"
Like this was the most important thing.
I started to say to him, "Okay!
But your job won't earn you your wings."

Then I overheard some chit chatter
Somebody said, "I'd rather be rich than poor."
But not one of those words really mattered
Because everybody dies and of that I'm sure.

You see what's really important in life
Is just one simple thing.
And that's accepting Jesus Christ
As your Savior, Lord, and King.

Silent Torture

Silent torture rules each day
While fires of desire burn within our souls.
The voices of messengers call out this way
But the question is which way do we go?

Horses from hell ride through the night.
The land lies still until their thunder comes.
The brain is the battlefield for the white and black knights.
Here comes the serpent's soldiers marching to the drum.

Lucifer is the loser but yet he's not losing.
Millions are unconcerned until their spirits burn.
The chosen weren't chosen at all to do the bruising.
God never said it was our turn.

War is waged on the sandy shores of the human mind.
Swords have been drawn each dedicated to death.
Blood trickles down a lance in a straight line.
In the eyes of a warrior are the corpses who are left.

The infantry moves into the dungeons of the heart
To unlock the doors and free the prisoners of pain.
But they can't see the locks because of the dark.
So they guide them with their voices to their locks and chains.

The key they use is hope it fits every single one.
The shackles fall from their wrists at the turn of the key.
As the captives ascend the stairs they see the glare of the Son.
The blood of Jesus and His only can make you free.

Sin

There's this feeling that's inside
That wants to get outside.
It's a feeling that we try but cannot always tie.

There's this longing in our souls
That wants to take control.
It's a longing we can't hold sometimes it just explodes.

It's not a fad.
It drives us mad.
It makes us do what's bad.

It's a vice
And it's not nice.
It makes us think things twice.

It's like a wind that twirls within.
It makes us just give in.
I'm talking about the struggle against sin.

Spirits

Things unseen are almost too often things misunderstood.
Not all of them are bad nor are all good.

We roam the earth conquering like ancient Rome's soldiers
But without detection.
Forcing our way around whatever comes in our direction.

Our goal is mass deception; we feel a need to deceive.
We are our own weapons; we don't want anyone to believe.

Who are we? We're the ghosts that haunt your house.
Who are we? We're the ones that make you doubt.

We enter your body through anger
And other negative emotions.
We rub right in like suntan lotion.

We help you conjure up and do everything that's wrong.
Then, after that, just like that. My man, we're gone.

You see we don't want to be around
When you suffer the consequences.
Don't try to figure us out. My man, it's senseless.

You see I am just one of many enemies of eternal life.
Me and the rest of my boys got kicked out of heaven
By Jesus Christ.

Stroke

My car needs brakes and tires.
And the sticker on my plate is about to expire.

I need my own computer but I don't have the cash.
Soon I'll be another commuter just flashing my bus pass.

Every dime I make goes on the bills.
This part I really hate because this is not my will.

So I turn on the T.V. to watch my favorite Al Bundy.
But ain't nothing funny when you don't have any money.

I owe everybody so they will never be broke.
If it wasn't for the Almighty I would've been had a stroke.

The Conversion

I was sixteen going on thirty
Just another teen on the path of destruction.
I use to indulge in everything that was dirty
Refusing to receive any kind of instruction.

Home invasion and strong-arm robbery
Were both games to this ghetto youth.
Pipedreams of me winning the lottery
I use to have till I found the truth.

I thought my role was to seek and molest her.
I guess you could say fornicator deluxe.
I've had seven hundred I was after Wilt's record
But he had the advantage cause he had the bucks.

I got a wakeup call just barely missed being dead.
I told the gang I wasn't going that day.
That's when my friend got shot in the head.
You see that bullet could've been meant for B.A.

I'm thirty-nine now going into eternity
Because I have accepted Christ.
You see Jesus died for you and me
So we could have eternal life.

The Cross

He was wounded for our transgressions
And with his scars we were healed.
He was the subject of Jewish oppression
And the lamb that Gentiles killed.

But it was the Lord who laid upon His son
The iniquity of us all.
His parents were warned by Simeon
Their child would rise then fall.

It pleased the Lord to bruise him
To make his soul a sacrifice for sin.
The Father had to choose him
He was the king through which men could win.

So he would tread the road to that place
Where he was impaled and held to the sun.
And there were smiles for awhile on every evil face
Until the deed was done.

So they killed the Prince of life
Without knowing he paid the cost.
But we'd all be lost if not for the Christ
Who died upon the cross.

The Flames Of Passion

The fire was trying to burn through
But I kept fanning back the flames of passion.
From the moment I saw her temptation grew
Cause she's the pearl behind the glass worth smashing.

I had been waiting for the opportunity to get her alone
So I could tell her of the crime I was guilty of.
So Satan suggested I slip her a poem
But I was convicted by the God of love who sits above.

But the devil was persistent.
He didn't just give up like that.
He put his arm around my back
And said, "Look at her Jack!

She's tall, she's stacked
And Baby girl, got back!"
He fans the flames of passion as I try to hold back.
Then he whispers, "I bet she even purrs like a cat."

He says, "Don't try to fight it.
Come on, you know you love it!"
Then I turn and recite,
"God said, 'Thou shalt not covet!'"

Then suddenly the flames of passion are smothered in a bowl.
You see in heaven's mansions
Are two mighty ones who can control
The flames of passion that burn in the human soul.

The Fool

He lifted up his eyes to heaven to mock Almighty God.
He said he found the story of creation strange and very odd.
So he opened up the Bible and he spat right on the scriptures.
Then he said, "I don't like books that do not have pictures."

He toyed around with Jesus, "Jesus this! Jesus that!"
Little did he know that God would play his life back.
Then the fool died that night and found himself before God.
He lost his sense of humor when he had to face the firing squad.

He fell down to his knees when he saw the king's face.
He started begging him for mercy but he found not God's grace.
As the scenes of his life were played back before all
He looked at the glow in the door of hell's hall.

Then an angel led him down a corridor to the lake of fire.
You see this will be the plight of all who make light of the Messiah.

The Forced Confession

They led him to a room with a two-way mirror,
And asked, "Where were you on the night of Nissan 14th?"
They showed him a picture of the world's only hero
As he sat there inside of this police precinct.

They promised he wouldn't be labeled a defector,
And asked, "Did you see the empty tomb the 1st of the week?"
He never gave his consent so they put away the lie detector.
Then another way to make him talk they had to seek.

That's when one struck him in the head with a telephone book.
Another punched him in the gut with his handcuffs.
When they held up the picture again and said, "Now look!"
That's was when his lunch gushed all over their stuff.

The captain said, "It's okay because everybody knows he's alive."
Then Satan covered his ears and yelled, "No, he's not! He died!"
Then Jesus touched him on his shoulder and he had to realize
That nothing can change the fact that the Lord did rise.

The Good Book

She claimed she couldn't stop smoking
So she kept lighting up, kept puffing and choking.
Then sure enough she was diagnosed with lung Cancer.

Then she blamed God for all her misery
And as she lay there asking, "Why me? Why me?"
The Good Book by her side had the answer.

He said he wanted sex without commitment
So over, and over he used his equipment.
Then finally he contracted the virus H.I.V.

A year ago a missionary handed him a little book.
He took the book but never gave it a look
And in that very book was how to stay Aids free.

There are those who say they believe in God
But what He's asking of me is just too hard.
These are they who worship wealth or self.

But when the judgment gavel comes crashing down
Those wicked smiles will be turned upside down.
Because He hasn't asked us to do anything
He hasn't done Himself.

I think it's time to get those Bibles off the shelf
Because there is no better book on self help.
And The Holy Bible even tells us how
We can cheat death.

The Good Father

I saw Father McCann he was scolding a man,
Saying, "Certain words shouldn't be heard
Around a child or woman."

The man took what he said
As he nodded his head.
And said, "Then I think it's about time you got going."

Then a drunk stumbled into the good father,
Who said, "Excuse me, I don't want to be a bother,
But is drinking then going gambling a sin?"

No, it's not! Is what he wanted to hear
As he stood there reeking of beer.
But then the father said, "Only if you never win."

Now the father was a real Bible lover
His has this beautiful black leather cover.
Those who saw him reading had all gathered around.

Then one said, "Attaboy, old chap!"
And he gave his back a slap
Then a centerfold from Playboy magazine fell to the ground.

There was a black that survived a collision
Who claimed he had a vision.
Who said, "I've been called to preach by the begotten."

He said, "I saw P.C. in a cloud!"
But the good father said, "Listen pal
For you that could only mean Pick Cotton!"

As the father preached his Sunday sermon.
He stood like Hitler before his Germans.
Then he saw something that made him stop his speech.

Then he said to this gray old fan,
"Hey you! Wake up, that man!"
But then the man said, "You wake him up!
You put him to sleep!"

The Grass Always Looks Greener

I feel like a broken bottle.
My life is shattered like pieces of glass everywhere.
But every fad I just had to follow
Cause I was caught up in the glitter and glare.

You know the long stretched limos the fancy sport cars
And the being seen at all the big movie events.
Where the Hollywood stars would laugh their hardy ha ha's
Seeing their names in bright lights and big print.

I was flirting with disaster
Around a starlet's neck was a string of pearls.
I took no heed to the warning master
Who said, "Love not the world."

Then into the ballroom entered the devil,
Full of flare, and looking debonair.
I knew I wasn't on his level
So I just held onto her chair.

He extended his ring-studded hand
As he did she gave a glance.
So I watched them as they danced before the band.
Because she agreed to dance this dance.

Then what we saw we couldn't believe.
You see they stole the show.
And I can't believe that I received
This kind of rigmarole.

Now his next move was just too clever.
He had his limousine waiting by the door.
Then I never and I mean ever
Saw my love no more.

You see she knew that she had found the one
Who could buy that string of pearls.
So what the devil had convinced me was fun
Would be what cost me my only girl.

I knew at that moment there in Argentina
I should've listened to the Prince of common sense.
You see the grass always looks greener
On the other side of the fence.

The Great Deceiver

He stood there like a golden statue
In the presence of the most high
As his eyes despised the Son of God
Sitting at his father's side.

His wings stretched across the very throne
He so badly wanted to sit upon.
But these seats were already taken
By a father and his son.

He use to sing to the glory of the very God
That he did hate.
His sinful thoughts would soon take shape
And he'd come to debate with God the great.

He kept entertaining the thought of being God
And that was when he fell.
So he rallied all his allies and a third of fools soon rebelled.
But he and his army had no win.
You see they were quickly expelled
And now he is leading the world in a mad stampede
Off the edge of a cliff
Into the fiery outstretched hands of hell.

And Lucifer won't stop deceiving
Until there is no one to deceive left.
You see the great deceiver was so good at deception
That he even deceived himself.

The Great God Jehovah

His name is called the Ancient of Days.
He sits on high knows all our ways.
His palace is the envy of all.
A chosen few shall be called.

His eyes of flame do roam the earth.
He brings about death and causes birth.
He waves His hand and stirs up the air.
Then showers rain from everywhere.

He blows His breath and brings the cold.
He owns the silver and the gold.
The life of man is in His hand.
He gave man breath and man began.

He made the birds; He made the trees.
He made their branches and their leaves.
He made the stars; He made the moon.
He forms the embryo inside the womb.

He made the water; He made the fire.
He saved us from slaughter when He gave us Messiah.
If He would cry all life would die.
We all should praise our God the Most High.

Because He sends His winds
And the flood waters come dashing over.
No one is as great as the great God Jehovah.

The Great White Throne

I rejoice at the thought
That God is going to repay them for their crime.
For years we have fought
And still were kept behind.

You see the doors were always shut
And so our hardships were caused.
We were in a rut
Because of their one-sided laws.

So it makes me happy to know
That not a single soul will escape.
For every word and every blow
The judgment of God now waits.

I get excited when I picture the great white throne
And the dead standing there before.
Where the secrets of men will be known
And where God will even the score.

I shout for joy when I think of Jesus Christ
And how he will expose every single liar.
You see those whose names aren't written in the book of life
Will be casted into the fire.

The Journey Called Life

I was walking down this long lonely road
In the rain, the heat, and the cold.

Fighting through the test called stress
While getting very little rest.

Living in hunger, despair, and pain
Trying to keep from going insane.

Dealing with all the vicious lies.
Looking away from her hypnotic eyes.

Chasing dreams that ran like streams.
Beholding things that weren't what they seemed.

Suffering from each failure that I was dealt
Trying to be that iceberg that didn't melt.

Yelling at the top of my voice.
Determined to tame that hardship horse.

Evaluating the thrills of worldly pleasure
And realizing each one was no real treasure.

Wishing I could just soar above like a dove
While searching for that thing called love.

Crying out for help to Jesus the Christ.
I'm talking about the journey called life.

The Keys Of Death And Hell

The great God who reigned deigned to save the human race.
His Son came in His name to spread about His grace.

The enemy engaged in rage when he saw earth's savior come.
He was mad and then sad because he couldn't keep him from.

Coming back from the land of black
He led the captives in a trail
As Jesus held in his hand the keys of death and hell.

He said, "Behold, I am he that was dead
And am alive forevermore."
And the enemy had to bow to him once more.

The Light

He was harboring some secret animosity
Because he knew what I was he needed to be.
He lived his life by his own twisted philosophy
But he knew deep inside he should be like me.

So he would look for every opportunity
To try to find something wrong with The Way.
He couldn't stand to see the unity in my community
And he didn't know someday he would still pay.

I started to say, "Instead of hating me for loving Christ.
You need to get on the road that is right!"
But instead I said, "Tonight for him I'll just pray
And hope that Jesus will show him The Light!"

The Lost

I can no longer see what's on the surface.
I now live in the land of the hopeless without a purpose.
The only color I can see is black.
I don't know which way I came so I won't be going back.

The sound of agony fills this cave
No one here is bold or brave.
The flames flare up all around.
The thick black smoke chokes and drowns.

Across from me I see the blessed and free
That is where I long to be but I can't go to them
And they can't come to me.

Regret stalks the chambers of my mind.
If only I had listened but I was blind.
The demons below mock constantly.
"You fool!" they say, "Now we're one big family!"

My tears dry before they leave my eyes
And my tongue feels like a sponge without moisture inside.
Time is now a mystery if only I had listened to thee.
If only I had listened! If only I had paid attention!

But now it's too late.
I must now burn forever in the fires of this lake.
I didn't have to be here if I would've believed in the cross.
You see under the green sponge lies the land of the lost.

The Miracle

I was coming home from the job
Then my car broke down.
When I bowed and prayed to God
There wasn't a soul around.

I was pushing my car I hadn't gotten too far
When a man volunteered to push mines with his.
So I quickly got back into my car
And this is exactly what he did.

He pushed me as far as he could
And then I told him thanks.
But after I thanked him for doing good
My car still wouldn't crank.

Then six other people
One by one would push my car with theirs.
And in this world of evil
I just knew this had to be The Man Upstairs.

Because the world we live in today
Is everything but spiritual.
As I walked in to stay
I knew it was a miracle.

The Moment You Die

I died and found myself standing
On the outside of this world
But right on the inside of death's door.

The door that was behind me could no longer be seen.
When I saw this breathtaking scene I thought it was a dream.

There were happy little children playing everywhere
Just running having fun without a single care.

Then I recalled the words Jesus spoke before he gave up his life.
He said, "Today, you will be with me in paradise."
But I had no idea that paradise would be this nice.

Then as the crowd towards me ran
On my shoulder laid a hand and when I turned to see the man.
I knew it was Father Abraham.

Yes, it was Father Abraham and I was sure.
He said, "Welcome to paradise, allow me to guide the tour."

He said, "Come enjoy this place till Jesus comes again.
You see this is what happens when you die my friend."

The Most Beautiful Verse

He shall descend into the flames like a moth.
He shall be consumed like a gasoline soaked clothe.
A fitting end for the Lord's only true rival.
Now let me tell you the most beautiful verse in the Bible.

But before I do think of all Satan has done.
Then I'm sure you will agree this is the one.
The verse is found in Revelation Chapter 20 verse 10
And for Lucifer it really is the perfect end.

Well at least to me there is no other scripture
That lifts my spirit higher.
It reads and the devil that deceived them
Was cast into the lake of fire.

The Rapture

I was walking down the street
When the clouds came tumbling down
That's when I realized my feet had left the ground.

I looked around and saw people gliding by
Being carried by the angels
To meet God in the sky.

I heard the trumpet sound it was the loudest I ever heard
And I was heaven-bound.
Literally, flying like a bird.

I noticed as the angels did fall
No one was trying to avoid being captured.
You see this is what we Christians call the rapture.

The Road

There's a road that has no stop signs
Nor does it have in its center a dividing line.

You can drive as fast as you want
Because there's no speed limit.
This road is not for the weak and timid.

On the sides of this road
It's okay to cheat on your wives and husbands.
All up and down the sides of this road
There are fornicators and adulterers by the dozens.

On this road it's okay to drink and drive.
It doesn't matter if you take a few people's lives.
On this road it's okay to use drugs
And to shoot out of your windows at rival gang thugs.

On this road it's okay to have an abortion.
On this road it's okay to kill and steal yourself a fortune.

On this road it's okay to be gay.
You don't have to hide. There are many here that way.

Now you might find this road exciting
But there's one more thing to tell
That this is the road that leads to hell.

The Unsung Heroes

I got my orders from The Light.
I spread my wings and took my flight.
I saw the assignment as I flew,
But she never had a clue.

That I was standing by her side
To help her out cause she had cried.
So I opened up her eyes and she saw the well,
I said, "The child shall survive
His strength won't fail."

She heard my words in her mind
But never saw a sight.
Then I returned full of joy to Jesus Christ.

You see the angel of the Lord encamps
Around the saints to keep them in the way.
We serve our God night and day
And we never seek applauds or any pay.

The psalmist wrote he makes His angels spirits
His ministers a flame of fire.
You see our only true desire
Is to serve our Lord the Messiah.

We are the soldiers of Jehovah
And we never covet.
We are the unsung heroes
And we're proud of it.

The Woman Who Believed

She came up behind them
With a heart filled with belief.
She knew if she could find him
She'd find relief.

The crowd was nice and thick
Around Israel's miracle working king.
For twelve years she had been sick
And to the physicians she had given everything.

So she forced her way through the crowd
When she saw the back of his robe.
Although the crowd was as thick as a cloud
She knew he could make her whole.

So she reached out in faith
And what she believed she did receive.
You see the blood was forced to abate
And never again would she ever bleed.

Because faith is the substance of things hoped for
And the evidence of things unseen.
You see this woman believed and she was sure
So she received that very thing.

This Is My Prayer

Lord keep me on the road that leads to eternal life.
Let me not turn to the left or the right.

Bring me to that door that leads to paradise.
This is my prayer in the name of Jesus Christ.

Those Who Do And Those Who Don't

They say we all love Jesus
But why are there so many pieces?
I mean after all there's only one Christ right?

They say our Church is the one that's true
But they don't do what God said do.
Somebody is not reading the Bible right.

They say we get our orders from The Man Upstairs
But the book He wrote they say is for squares.
The Bible says He will but they say He won't.

Let me break it down. Let me end this story.
You see there are really just two categories.
Those who do and those who don't.

Thou Shalt Not Steal

The thief just couldn't resist the temptation
To keep some of the enemy spoil.
He knew what God said to the nation
But the tempter had come to foil.

He kept looking at that Babylonian garment.
It was one of the finest ever made,
So finally he disregarded everything his Lord had said.

So he rolled up the garment and strolled into his tent.
He dug a hole in the earth and in the garment went.
And he really thought that would be the end of it.

But then the nation lost its first battle
And the people started to complain.
Then the Lord revealed why to their leader
As they all stood there in pain.

So Joshua asked Achan if he had stolen
And to this, he said, "It's true."
Then Joshua said, "You have troubled Israel
And now Israel shall trouble you."

So they took Achan and his family out by the gate
Where they were stoned to death but all the people.
As they shouted, "God said, 'Thou shalt not steal.'
In His eyes this is evil.'"

What Are You Going To Do?

Christ started a fire
The devil tried to put it out
But it caught onto his shoes.

All who died
And became martyrs for Jesus Christ.
Won! They didn't lose.

One day, this same trial may come to you
And if it does
What are you going to do?

You Always Have A Choice

If I should die before my time;
Please, don't cry for me.
You see I made Jesus mines;
Therefore, I got the victory.

If I should pass by some violent crime;
Please, don't weep or moan
Just picture me in your mind
On my way back home.

If I should depart in some way that's bad;
Please, don't shed no tears
Just think of what we had.
Think back on those good years.

Don't sob before my casket sitting
Cause I accepted Christ.
Save those tears for the ones who didn't
Who will never see paradise.

I don't want you to weep at my funeral;
Instead, I want you to rejoice.
Because of Christ I want you to know;
You always have a choice.

You Reap What You Sow

I've been here for fifteen years waiting
Only through the bars I can see the sun.
I live in a constant state of expectation.

I've seen on television the hating.
The people reminding me of what I've done.
They're debating my case all across the nation.

I knew one day I would hear my cell unlock
And the footsteps of those who came in.
I knew someday the clock would stop
And the reaper's work would begin.

So when that day came I made my peace
With The Man Upstairs and not a moment too soon.
They told me the governor had exclaimed,
"No!" to my release so they escorted me to that room.

They strapped me to the table;
After, I had finished my last meal.
I thought if I were able;
I'd go back and choose not to kill.

Then I watched as the poison was ejected
From the needle in the executioner's hand.
As scenes of my life were being projected
From when I was a boy to now a man.

Then I could feel myself becoming sleepy
As my eyes closed very slow.
Then I remembered my daddy use to preach to me
You reap what you sow.

CPSIA information can be obtained
at www.ICGtesting.com
Printed in the USA
BVHW030646280922
648109BV00008B/179